Homes in Colonial America

By Mark Thomas

Welcome
Books

Children's Press®
A Division of Scholastic Inc.
New York / Toronto / London / Auckland / Sydney
Mexico City / New Delhi / Hong Kong
Danbury, Connecticut

Photo Credits: Cover © Richard T. Nowitz/Corbis; pp. 5, 7, 9, 11, 13, 15, 17, 19 © Colonial Williamsburg Foundation; p. 21 © Wendell Metzell/Index Stock Imagery
Contributing Editor: Jennifer Silate
Book Design: Erica Clendening

Library of Congress Cataloging-in-Publication Data

Thomas, Mark, 1963—
Homes in Colonial America / by Mark Thomas.
    p. cm. — (Colonial America)
Includes index.
Summary: Simple text and photographs depict homes in Colonial America, describing their interiors, exteriors, and such typical features as fireplaces and outhouses.
ISBN 0-516-23933-3 (lib. bdg.) — ISBN 0-516-23493-5 (pbk.)
1. Architecture, domestic—United States—Juvenile literature. 2. Architecture, Colonial—United States—Juvenile literature. 3. United States—History—Colonial period, ca. 1600–1775—Juvenile literature. [1. Architecture, Domestic—History. 2. Architecture, Colonial. 3. Dwellings—History. 4. United States—Social life and customs—1600–1775.] I. Title. II. Colonial America (Children's Press)

NA707 .T48 2002
728'.0973'09032—dc21

2001037107

Contents

1 Colonial American Homes   4

2 Fireplaces   12

3 Kitchens   18

4 New Words   22

5 To Find Out More   23

6 Index   24

7 About the Author   24

There were many kinds of homes in **Colonial America**.

Most homes were made of wood.

Some wooden homes were made out of logs.

They are called **log cabins**.

7

Some homes in Colonial
America were made
of **brick**.

Brick homes are very strong.

9

Most of the **furniture** in Colonial American homes was made of wood.

11

Homes in Colonial America had **fireplaces**.

Fireplaces were made of brick.

13

Wood was burned in the fireplace.

The fire kept people warm.

It also gave light.

15

People used candles for light, too.

Many homes in Colonial America did not have **kitchens**.

The kitchen was in another **building**.

19

We can still visit homes from Colonial America today.

21

New Words

brick (**brihk**) a block of baked clay that is used to build things

building (**bihl**-dihng) a place where people live or work, like a house

Colonial America (kuh-**loh**-nee-uhl uh-**mer**-uh-kuh) the time before the United States became a country (1620–1780)

fireplaces (**fyr**-play-suhz) stone or brick areas where it is safe to have a fire

furniture (**fer**-nuh-chuhr) objects in a house, like beds, chairs, tables, and desks

kitchens (**kihch**-uhns) rooms where food is prepared or cooked

log cabins (**lawg cab**-ihns) small houses made out of logs

To Find Out More

Books
The Early Family Home
by Bobbie D. Kalman
Crabtree Publishing

If You Lived at the Time of the American Revolution
by Kay Moore
Scholastic Trade

Web Site
Colonial Kids: Our Home
http://library.thinkquest.org/J002611F/house.htm
You can learn a lot about homes in Colonial America on this site. See where people lived. Find out how they slept, kept warm, and cooked.

Index

candles, 16

brick, 8, 12
building, 18

fireplace, 12, 14

furniture, 10

kitchen, 18

light, 14, 16
log cabins, 6

wood, 4, 10, 14

About the Author
Mark Thomas has written more than fifty children's and young adult books. He writes and teaches in Florida.

Reading Consultants
Kris Flynn, Coordinator, Small School District Literacy, The San Diego County Office of Education

Shelly Forys, Certified Reading Recovery Specialist, W.J. Zahnow Elementary School, Waterloo, IL

Sue McAdams, Former President of the North Texas Reading Council of the IRA, and Early Literacy Consultant, Dallas, TX

4/1   2 circ (bl a4)